Magnet Board Creations
in Plastic Canvas

I0893018

LEISURE ARTS, INC. • Maumelle, Arkansas

Contents

merry little

• MAGNET BOARD CREATIONS •
PLASTIC CANVAS

Happy Valentine's Day

LOVEBUG

Size: 4¼"w x 4"h

Supplies: Worsted weight yarn (refer to color key), one 10½" x 13½" sheet of clear 7 mesh plastic canvas, #16 tapestry needle, two 10mm moveable eyes, one ½" red pom-pom, 2½" length of black cloth-covered floral wire, 8" length of ¼"w red ribbon, two 3" lengths of 3mm red chenille stem, magnetic strip, and craft glue.

Instructions

1. Follow charts to cut and stitch Lovebug pieces.
2. Tack Wings to back of Body.
3. Glue eyes, pom-pom, and wire to Body. Trim wire ends.
4. Tie bow with ribbon; glue bow to Body. Trim ends.
5. Glue chenille stems to back of Body; shape as desired.
6. Glue magnetic strip to back of Body.

Color Key
- White
- Red

Wings
(11 x 11 threads)
(stitch 2)

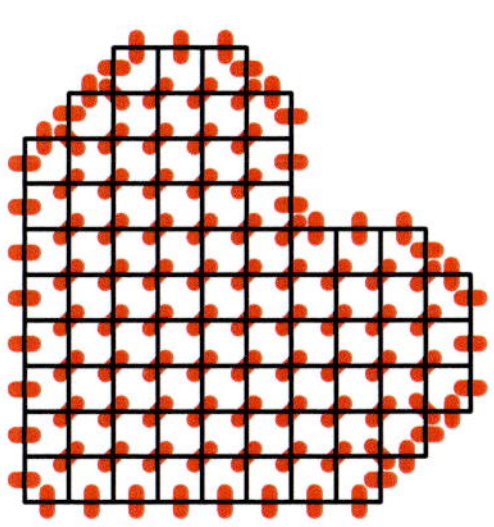

Body
(15 x 19 threads)

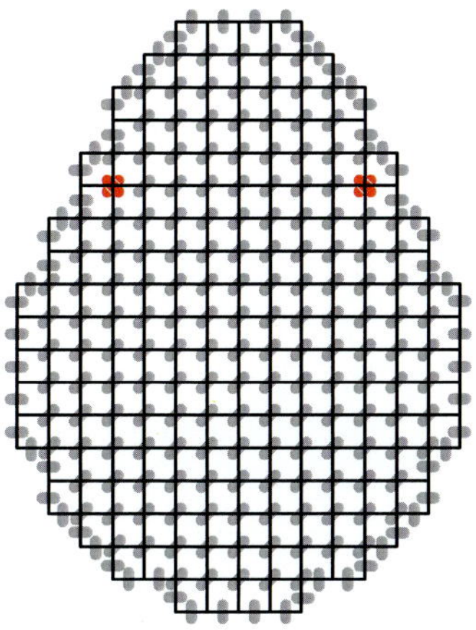

Happy St. Patrick's Day

LEPRECHAUN

Size: 2½"w x 4"h

Supplies: Worsted weight yarn (refer to color key), one 10½" x 13½" sheet of clear 7 mesh plastic canvas, #16 tapestry needle, two 10mm moveable eyes, one ½" orange pom-pom, 2½" length of black cloth-covered floral wire, 8" length of ¼"w orange ribbon, magnetic strip, and craft glue.

Instructions

1. Follow charts to cut and stitch Leprechaun pieces.

2. Tack Buckle to Hat. Tack Hat to Body.

3. Glue eyes, pom-pom, and wire to Body. Trim wire ends.

4. Tie bow with ribbon; glue bow to Body. Trim ends.

5. Glue magnetic strip to back of Body.

Color Key

- Yellow
- Orange
- Flesh
- Dark Pink
- Light Green
- Green

Buckle
(6 x 6 threads)

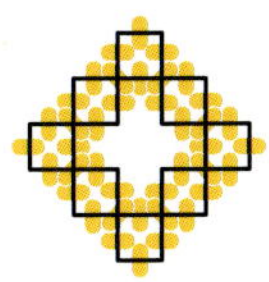

Hat
(16 x 12 threads)

Body
(15 x 19 threads)

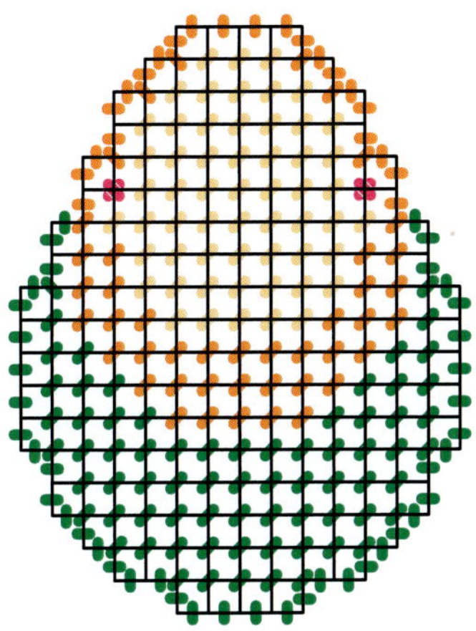

Happy Easter

BUNNY

Size: 2¾"w x 4¼"h

Supplies: Worsted weight yarn (refer to color key), one 10½" x 13½" sheet of clear 7 mesh plastic canvas, #16 tapestry needle, two 10mm moveable eyes, two 2¾" lengths of white cloth-covered floral wire, one ½" pink pom-pom, two 1¼" lengths of black cloth-covered floral wire, 8" length of ¼"w yellow ribbon, magnetic strip, and craft glue.

Instructions

1. Follow charts to cut and stitch Bunny pieces.
2. Tack Ears to back of Body.
3. Glue eyes and black wires to Body. Trim wire ends.
4. Glue white wires and pom-pom to Body. Trim wire ends.
5. Tie bow with ribbon; glue bow to Body. Trim ends.
6. Glue magnetic strip to back of Body.

Color Key
- White
- Pink

Ear
(11 x 11 threads)
(stitch 2)

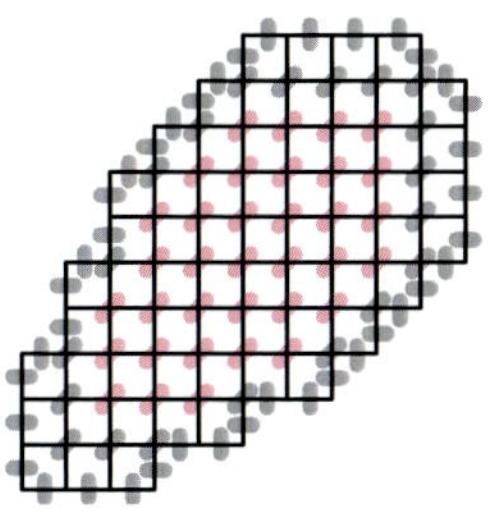

Body
(15 x 19 threads)

CHICK

Size: 3¼"w x 3¾"h

Supplies: Worsted weight yarn (refer to color key), one 10½" x 13½" sheet of clear 7 mesh plastic canvas, #16 tapestry needle, two 10mm moveable eyes, one yellow feather, 8" length of ¼"w pink ribbon, magnetic strip, and craft glue.

Instructions

1. Follow charts to cut and stitch Chick pieces, working French knots last.
2. Tack top edge of Beak and Wings to Body.
3. Glue eyes to Body.
4. Glue feather to back of Body.
5. Tie bow with ribbon; glue bow to Body. Trim ends.
6. Glue magnetic strip to back of Body.

Color Key

- Yellow
- Orange
- Dark Pink
- Light Green (French Knot)

Beak
(6 x 6 threads)

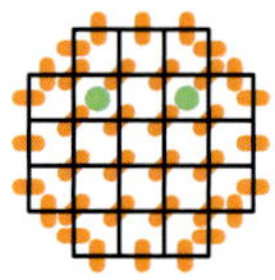

Body
(15 x 19 threads)

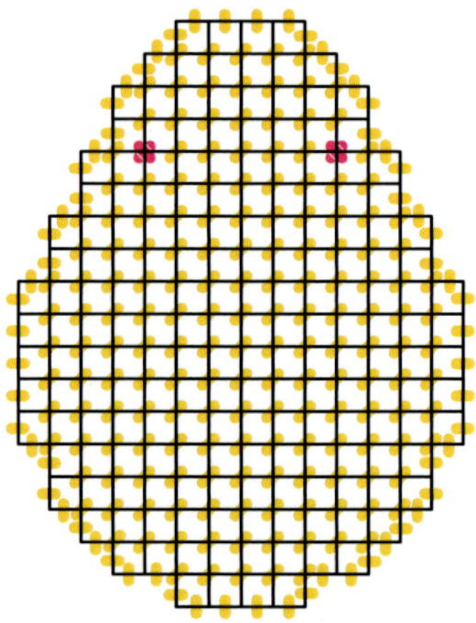

Left Wing
(8 x 8 threads)

Right Wing
(8 x 8 threads)

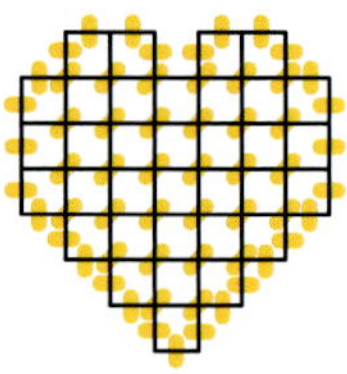

EGG

Size: 2¼"w x 2¾"h

Supplies: Worsted weight yarn (refer to color key), one 10½" x 13½" sheet of clear 7 mesh plastic canvas, #16 tapestry needle, two 10mm moveable eyes, one ¼" yellow pom-pom, 2½" length of black cloth-covered floral wire, 8" length of ¼"w pink ribbon, magnetic strip, and craft glue.

Instructions

1. Follow chart to cut and stitch Egg piece, working French knots last.
2. Glue eyes, pom-pom, and wire to Body. Trim wire ends.
3. Tie bow with ribbon; glue bow to Body. Trim ends.
4. Glue magnetic strip to back of Body.

Color Key

- White
- Yellow
- Pink
- Light Green
- Light Green (French Knot)

Body
(15 x 19 threads)

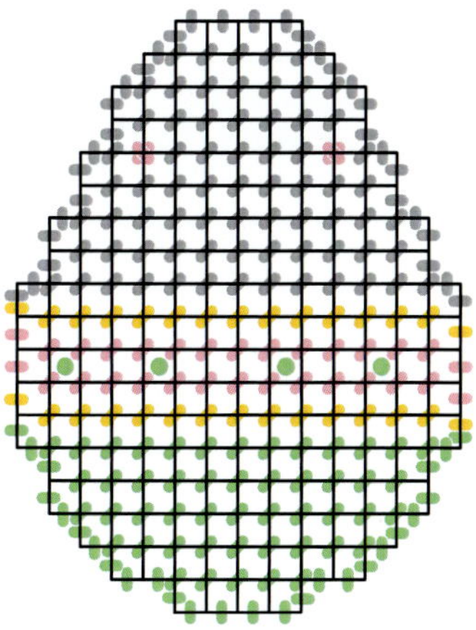

Lemon-Blueberry Bread

• MAGNET BOARD CREATIONS •

PLASTIC CANVAS

Happy July 4th

UNCLE SAM

Size: 2¼"w x 4"h

Supplies: Worsted weight yarn (refer to color key), one 10½" x 13½" sheet of clear 7 mesh plastic canvas, #16 tapestry needle, two 10mm moveable eyes, one ½" red pom-pom, 2½" length of black cloth-covered floral wire, 8" length of ¼"w red ribbon, magnetic strip, and craft glue.

Instructions

1. Follow charts to cut and stitch Uncle Sam pieces, working French knots last.
2. Tack Hat to Body.
3. Glue eyes, pom-pom, and wire to Body. Trim wire ends.
4. Tie bow with ribbon; glue bow to Body. Trim ends.
5. Glue magnetic strip to back of Body.

Color Key

- White
- Flesh
- Red
- Blue
- Yellow (French Knot)

Hat
(15 x 10 threads)

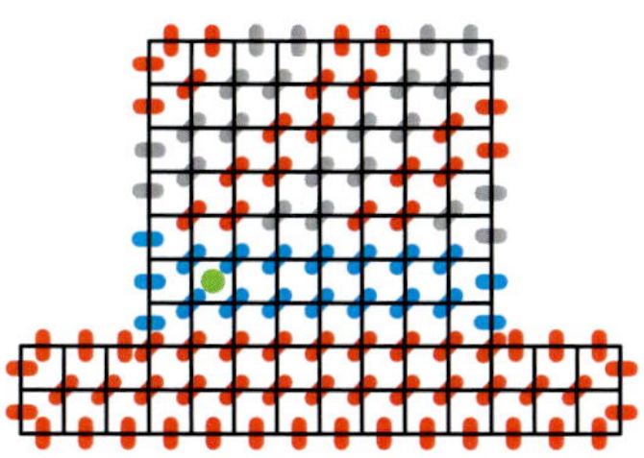

Body
(15 x 19 threads)

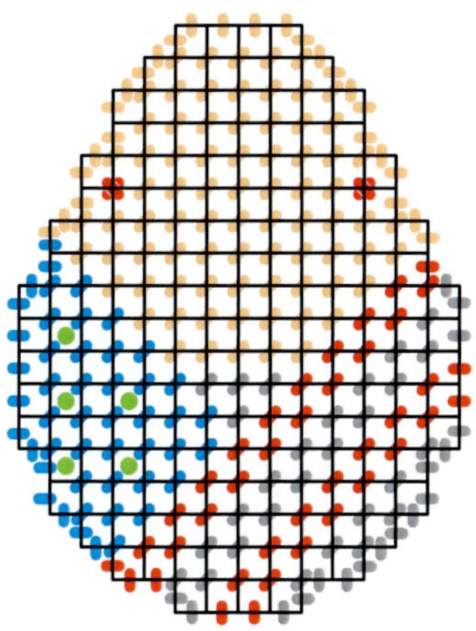

BUNCH
Thank you
THANKS

Happy Halloween

WITCH

Size: 3"w x 4¼"h

Supplies: Worsted weight yarn (refer to color key), one 10½" x 13½" sheet of clear 7 mesh plastic canvas, #16 tapestry needle, two 10mm moveable eyes, one ¼" pink pom-pom, 2" length of black cloth-covered floral wire, 8" length of ¼"w orange ribbon, magnetic strip, and craft glue.

Instructions

1. Follow charts to cut and stitch Witch pieces, working French knots last.
2. For hair, cut four 4" lengths of orange yarn. Fold each strand of yarn in half and glue fold to back of Hat. Tack Hat to Body. Trim yarn ends.
3. Glue eyes, pom-pom, and wire to Body. Trim wire ends.
4. Tie bow with ribbon; glue bow to Body. Trim ends.
5. Glue magnetic strip to back of Body.

Color Key

- Orange
- Light Pink
- Dark Pink
- Black
- Orange (French Knot)

Hat
(17 x 14 threads)

Body
(15 x 19 threads)

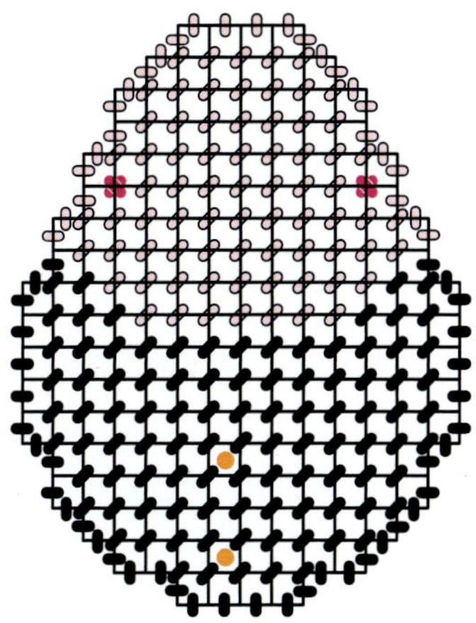

SPIDER

Size: 5"w x 3"h

Supplies: Worsted weight yarn (refer to color key), one 10½" x 13½" sheet of clear 7 mesh plastic canvas, #16 tapestry needle, two 10mm moveable eyes, one ¼" orange pom-pom, one 2½" length of orange cloth-covered floral wire, eight 6½" lengths of black cloth-covered floral wire, 8" length of ¼"w orange ribbon, magnetic strip, and craft glue.

Instructions

1. Follow charts to cut and stitch Spider pieces.
2. Glue eyes, pom-pom, and orange wire to Body. Trim wire ends.
3. For each leg, bend one black wire length in half. Twist two sides of folded wire together. Glue one end of wire to back of Body. Glue remaining end to back of Foot.
4. Tie bow with ribbon; glue bow to Body. Trim ends.
5. Glue magnetic strip to back of Body.

Color Key
- Orange
- Black

Left Foot
(6 x 5 threads)
(stitch 4)

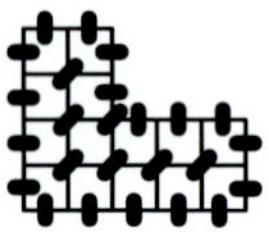

Right Foot
(6 x 5 threads)
(stitch 4)

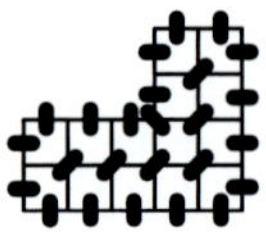

Body
(15 x 19 threads)

CANDY CORN

Size: 2¼"w x 2¾"h

Supplies: Worsted weight yarn (refer to color key), one 10½" x 13½" sheet of clear 7 mesh plastic canvas, #16 tapestry needle, two 10mm moveable eyes, one ¼" orange pom-pom, 4¼" length of black cloth-covered floral wire, 8" length of ¼"w orange ribbon, magnetic strip, and craft glue.

Instructions

1. Follow chart to cut and stitch Candy Corn piece.

2. Glue eyes and pom-pom to Body.

3. For mouth, shape wire and glue to Body. Trim ends.

4. Tie bow with ribbon; glue bow to Body. Trim ends.

5. Glue magnetic strip to back of Body.

Color Key

- White
- Yellow
- Orange

Body
(15 x 19 threads)

CAT

Size: 2½"w x 3¼"h

Supplies: Worsted weight yarn (refer to color key), one 10½" x 13½" sheet of clear 7 mesh plastic canvas, #16 tapestry needle, two 10mm moveable eyes, orange cloth-covered floral wire, one ¼" orange pom-pom, 8" length of ¼"w orange ribbon, magnetic strip, and craft glue.

Instructions

1. Follow charts to cut and stitch Cat pieces.
2. Tack Ears to back of Body.
3. Glue eyes to Body.
4. For mouth, cut two 1½" lengths of wire. Glue wire to Body. Trim wire ends.
5. For whiskers, cut three 2½" lengths of wire. Glue wire to Body; trim ends. Glue pom-pom to Body.
6. Tie bow with ribbon; glue bow to Body. Trim ends.
7. Glue magnetic strip to back of Body.

Color Key

- Orange
- Black

Ear
(6 x 6 threads)
(stitch 2)

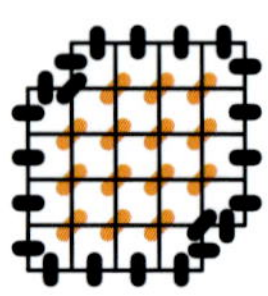

Body
(15 x 19 threads)

. MAGNET BOARD CREATIONS .
PLASTIC CANVAS

Happy Thanksgiving

PILGRIM

Size: 3"w x 3¾"h

Supplies: Worsted weight yarn (refer to color key), one 10½" x 13½" sheet of clear 7 mesh plastic canvas, #16 tapestry needle, 12" length of dk brown yarn, two 10mm moveable eyes, one ¼" pink pom-pom, two 5mm black pom-poms, 2" length of black cloth-covered floral wire, 8" length of ¼"w orange ribbon, magnetic strip, and craft glue.

Instructions

1. Follow charts to cut and stitch Pilgrim pieces, working backstitches last.
2. For hair, cut six 2" lengths of dk brown yarn. Fold each strand of yarn in half and glue fold to back of Hat. Tack Hat to Body. Trim yarn ends.
3. Glue eyes, pom-poms, and wire to Body. Trim wire ends.
4. Tie bow with ribbon; glue bow to Body. Trim ends.
5. Glue magnetic strip to back of Body.

Color Key

- White
- Orange
- Light Pink
- Dark Pink
- Brown
- Black

Hat
(15 x 9 threads)

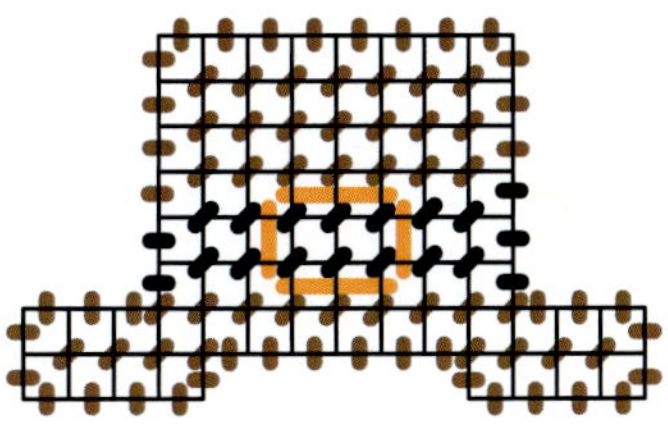

Body
(15 x 19 threads)

TURKEY

Size: 4¼"w x 4"h

Supplies: Worsted weight yarn (refer to color key), one 10½" x 13½" sheet of clear 7 mesh plastic canvas, #16 tapestry needle, two 10mm moveable eyes, 8" length of ¼"w orange ribbon, magnetic strip, and craft glue.

Instructions

1. Follow charts to cut and stitch Turkey pieces.
2. Tack top edge of Beak and Wattle to Body.
3. Tack Feathers to back of Body.
4. Glue eyes to Body.
5. Tie bow with ribbon; glue bow to Body. Trim ends.
6. Glue magnetic strip to back of Body.

Color Key

- Yellow
- Orange
- Red
- Green
- Brown

Body
(15 x 19 threads)

Beak
(6 x 5 threads)

Wattle
(9 x 9 threads)

Feather
(9 x 9 threads)

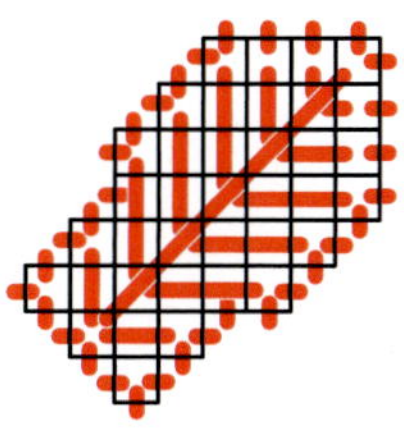

Feather
(9 x 9 threads)
(stitch 2)

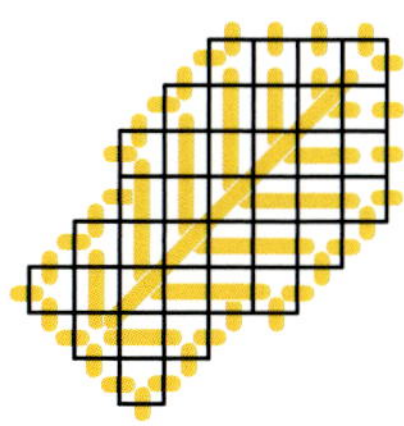

Feather
(9 x 9 threads)
(stitch 2)

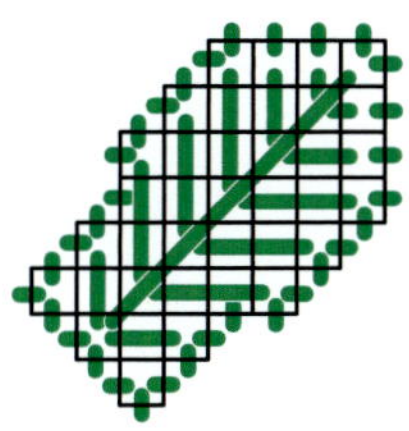

Feather
(9 x 9 threads)
(stitch 2)

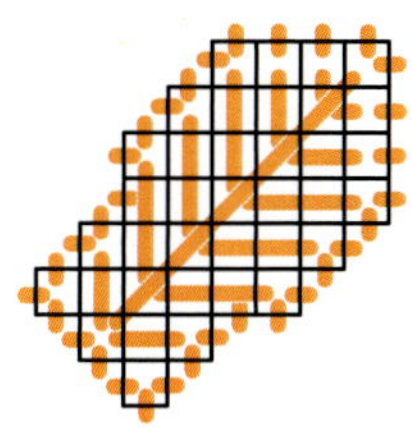

WISHING YOU A
merry little

Merry Christmas

SNOWMAN

Size: 4¼"w x 3¾"h

Supplies: Worsted weight yarn (refer to color key), one 10½" x 13½" sheet of clear 7 mesh plastic canvas, #16 tapestry needle, two 10mm moveable eyes, 2" length of black cloth-covered floral wire, 8" length of ¼"w blue ribbon, magnetic strip, and craft glue.

Instructions

1. Follow charts to cut and stitch Snowman pieces, working French knot last.
2. Tack top edge of Nose to Body.
3. Tack Flower to Hat. Tack Hat to Body.
4. Tack Arms to back of Body.
5. Glue eyes and wire to Body. Trim wire ends.
6. Tie bow with ribbon; glue bow to Body. Trim ends.
7. Glue magnetic strip to back of Body.

Color Key

- White
- Yellow
- Orange
- Red
- Blue
- Brown
- Black
- Red (French Knot)

Hat
(14 x 9 threads)

Body
(15 x 19 threads)

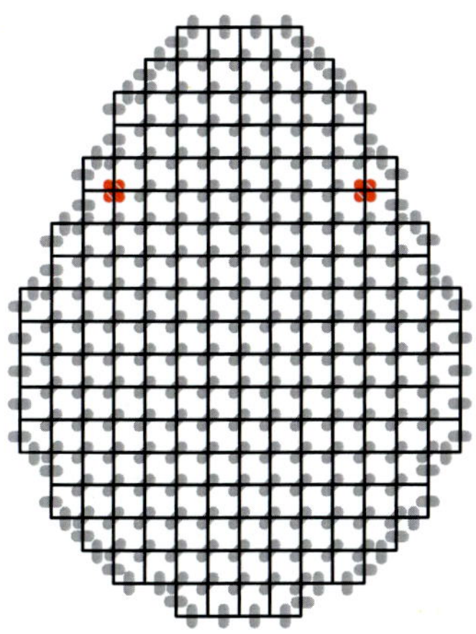

Flower
(4 x 4 threads)

Nose
(4 x 5 threads)

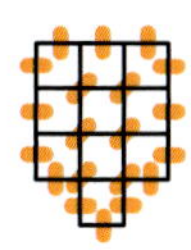

Left Arm
(8 x 11 threads)

Right Arm
(8 x 11 threads)

REINDEER

Size: 3¾"w x 4¼"h

Supplies: Worsted weight yarn (refer to color key), one 10½" x 13½" sheet of clear 7 mesh plastic canvas, #16 tapestry needle, two 10mm moveable eyes, one ½" red pom-pom, 2¾" length of black cloth-covered floral wire, 8" length of ¼"w red ribbon, magnetic strip, and craft glue.

Instructions

1. Follow charts to cut and stitch Reindeer pieces.

2. Tack Antlers and Ears to back of Body.

3. Glue eyes, pom-pom, and wire to Body. Trim wire ends.

4. Tie bow with ribbon; glue bow to Body. Trim ends.

5. Glue magnetic strip to back of Body.

Color Key

- Yellow
- Red
- Tan
- Brown

Ear
(8 x 8 threads)
(stitch 2)

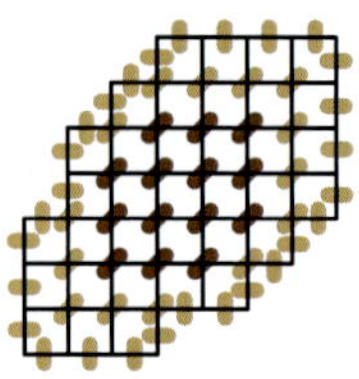

Body
(15 x 19 threads)

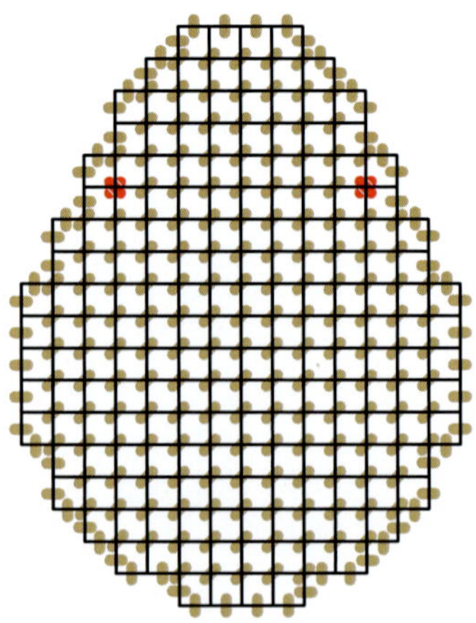

Antler
(11 x 13 threads)
(stitch 2)

ANGEL

Size: 4¼"w x 3¾"h

Supplies: Worsted weight yarn (refer to color key), one 10½" x 13½" sheet of clear 7 mesh plastic canvas, #16 tapestry needle, two 10mm moveable eyes, one ¼" pink pom-pom, 2" length of black cloth-covered floral wire, 8" length of ¼"w pink ribbon, one 4½" length of 3mm metallic gold chenille stem, magnetic strip, and craft glue.

Instructions

1. Follow charts to cut and stitch Angel pieces.
2. Tack Hair to Body.
3. Tack Wings to back of Body.
4. Glue eyes, pom-pom, and wire to Body. Trim wire ends.
5. Tie bow with ribbon; glue bow to Body. Trim ends.
6. For halo, shape halo and glue chenille stem end to back of Body.
7. Glue magnetic strip to back of Body.

Color Key

- White
- Yellow
- Flesh
- Red

Hair
(13 x 10 threads)

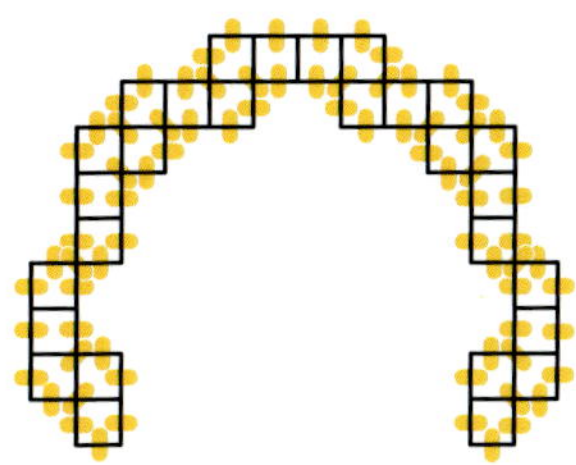

Wing
(11 x 12 threads)
(stitch 2)

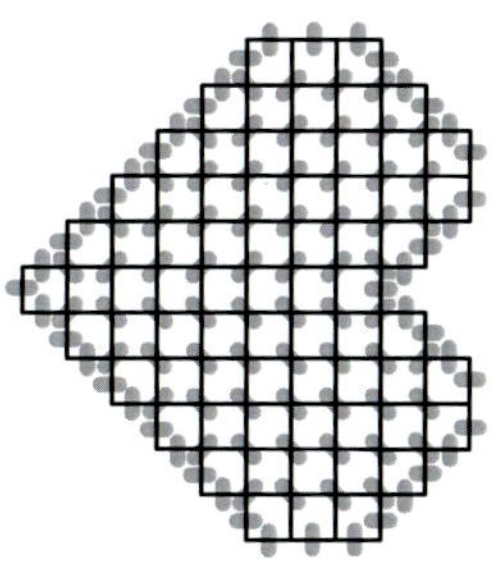

Body
(15 x 19 threads)

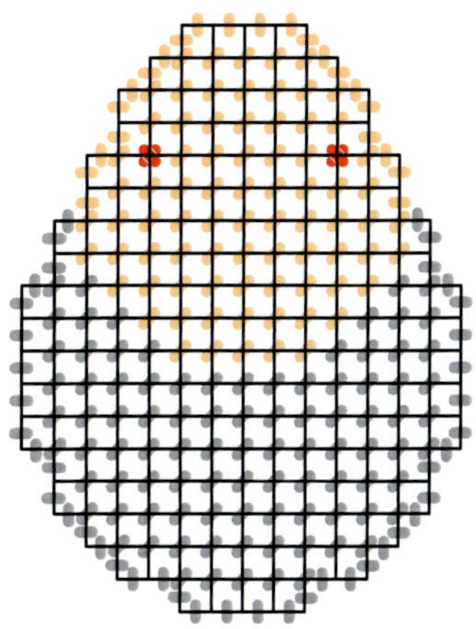

General Instructions

Plastic Canvas Basics

Working With Plastic Canvas

Counting Threads. Throughout this leaflet, the lines of the canvas will be referred to as threads. However, they are not actually "threads" since the canvas is not woven. Before cutting out your pieces, note the thread count of each chart. The thread count is listed above the chart and indicates the number of threads in the width and height of the canvas pieces. To cut plastic canvas pieces accurately, count threads (not holes) as shown in ***Fig. 1***.

Marking the Canvas. If you find it necessary to mark on the canvas, use an overhead projector pen. Outline shape with pen, cut out shape, and remove markings with water and a towel.

Cutting the Canvas. When cutting canvas, make sure to cut as close to the thread as possible without cutting into the thread. If you don't cut close enough, "nubs" or "pickets" will be left on the edge of your canvas. Make sure to cut off all nubs from the canvas before you begin to stitch because nubs will snag the yarn and are difficult to cover. A craft knife is helpful when cutting a small area from the center of a larger piece of canvas. When using a craft knife, protect the table below your canvas with a layer of cardboard or a magazine.

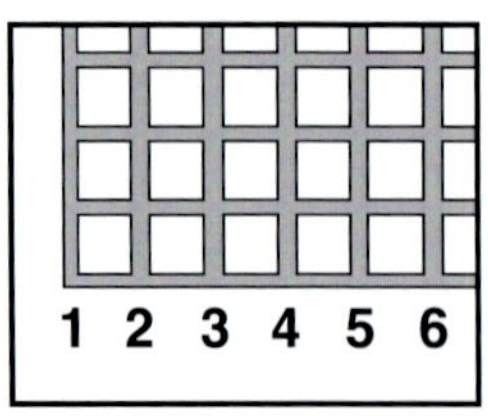

Fig. 1

Working With Yarn

Selecting Yarn. We used various brands of worsted weight yarn to stitch the photography models for this leaflet.

Dye Lot Variations. It is important to buy all of the yarn you need to complete your project from the same dye lot. Although variations in color may be slight when yarns from two different dye lots are held together, the variation is usually apparent on a stitched piece.

Reading The Color Key

Color keys are included for each project. The key indicates the colors of yarn used and how each color is represented on the chart. For example, when white yarn is represented by a grey line in the color key, all grey stitches on the chart should be stitched using white yarn.

Reading The Chart

Whenever possible, the drawing on the chart looks like the completed stitch. For example, the tent stitches on the chart are drawn diagonally across one intersection of threads just like tent stitches look on your piece of canvas. When a stitch cannot clearly be drawn on the chart, like a French knot, a symbol will be used instead. If you have difficulty determining how a particular stitch is worked, refer to Stitch Diagrams on pages 27–28.

Stitching The Design

Securing the First Stitch. Don't knot the end of your yarn before you begin stitching. Instead, begin each length of yarn by coming up from the wrong side of the canvas and leaving a 1"–2" tail on the wrong side. Hold this tail against the canvas and work the first few stitches over the tail.

When secure, clip the tail close to your stitched piece. Clipping the tail closely is important because long tails can become tangled in future stitches or can show through to the right side of the canvas.

Using Even Tension. Keep your stitching tension consistent, with each stitch lying flat and even on the canvas. Pulling or yanking the yarn causes the tension to be too tight, and you will be able to see through your project. Loose tension is caused by not pulling the yarn firmly enough, and the yarn will not lie flat on the canvas.

Ending Your Stitches. After you've completed all of the stitches of one color in an area, end your stitching by running your needle under several stitches on the back of the stitched piece. To keep the tails of the yarn from showing through or becoming tangled in future stitches, trim the end of the yarn close to the stitched piece.

Stitching Tips

Length of Yarn. It is best to begin stitching with a piece of yarn that is approximately one yard long. However, when working large areas of the same color, you may want to begin with a longer length of yarn to reduce the number of yarn ends and keep the back of your project looking neat.

Keeping Stitches Smooth. Most stitches tend to twist the yarn. Drop your needle and let the yarn untwist every few stitches or whenever needed.

Joining Pieces

Tacking. To tack pieces, run your needle under the backs of some stitches on one stitched piece to secure the yarn. Then run your needle through the canvas or under the stitches on the piece to be tacked in place. The idea is to securely attach your pieces without your tacking stitches showing.

Stitch Diagrams

Unless otherwise indicated, bring threaded needle up at **1** *and all* **odd** *numbers and down at* **2** *and all* **even** *numbers.*

Tent Stitch

This stitch is worked in horizontal or vertical rows over one intersection as shown in ***Fig. 2***. Refer to ***Fig. 3*** to work the reversed tent stitch.

Gobelin Stitch

This basic straight stitch is worked over two or more threads or intersections ***(Fig. 4)***. The number of threads or intersections may vary according to the chart.

Cross Stitch

This stitch is composed of two stitches ***(Fig. 5)***. The top stitch of each cross must always be made in the same direction.

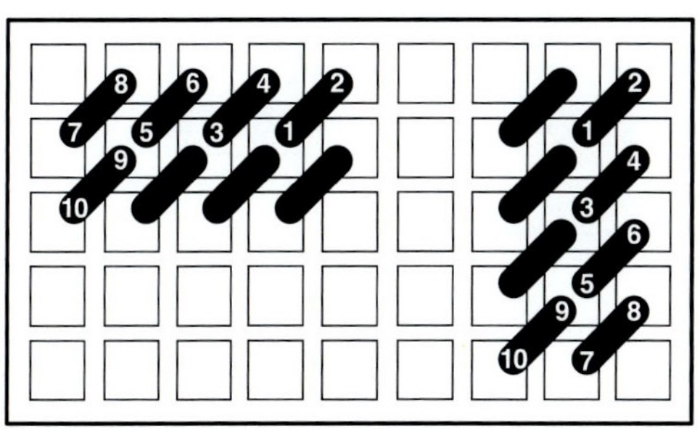

Fig. 2

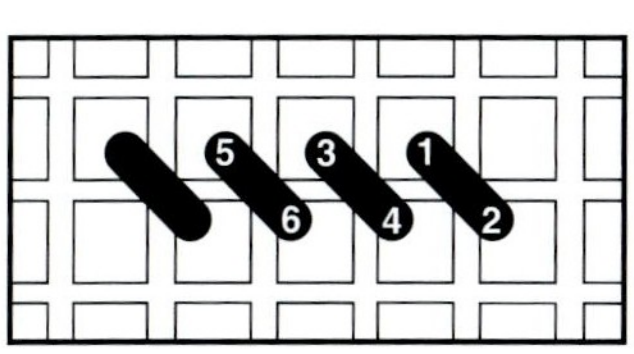

Fig. 3

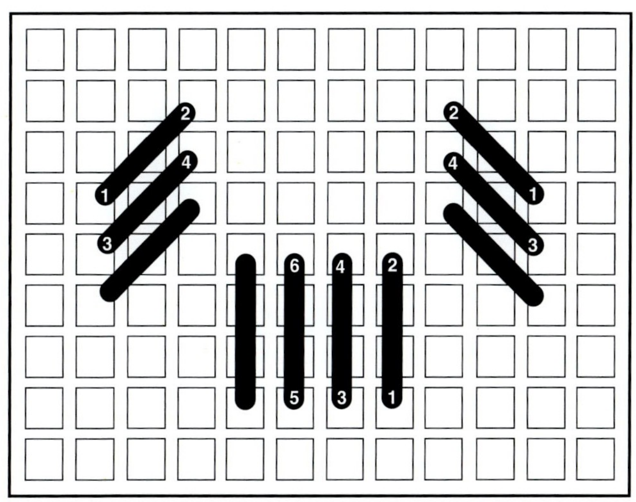

Fig. 4

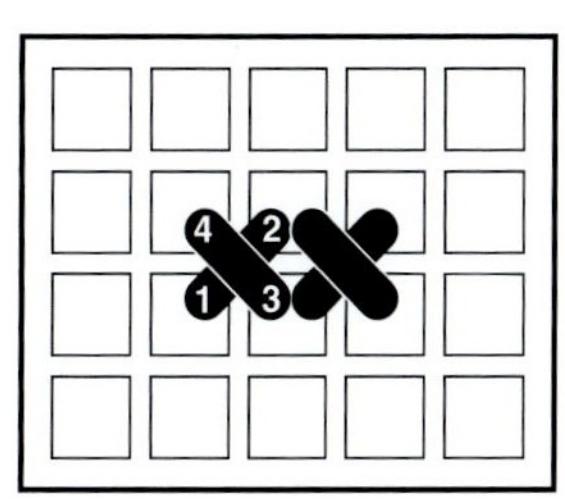

Fig. 5

Smyrna Cross Stitch

This stitch is worked over two threads as a decorative stitch. Each stitch is worked completely before going on to the next stitch ***(Fig. 6)***.

Backstitch

This stitch is worked over completed stitches to outline or define ***(Fig. 7)***. It is sometimes worked over more than one thread.

French Knot

Come up at 1. Wrap yarn once around needle. Insert the needle at 2 and pull it through the canvas, holding the yarn until it must be released ***(Fig. 8)***.

Overcast Stitch

This stitch covers the edge of the canvas ***(Fig. 9)***. It may be necessary to go through the same hole more than once to get even coverage on the edge, especially at the corners.

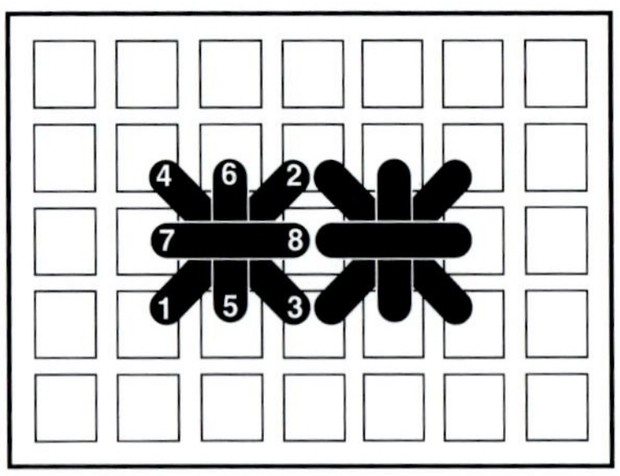

Fig. 6

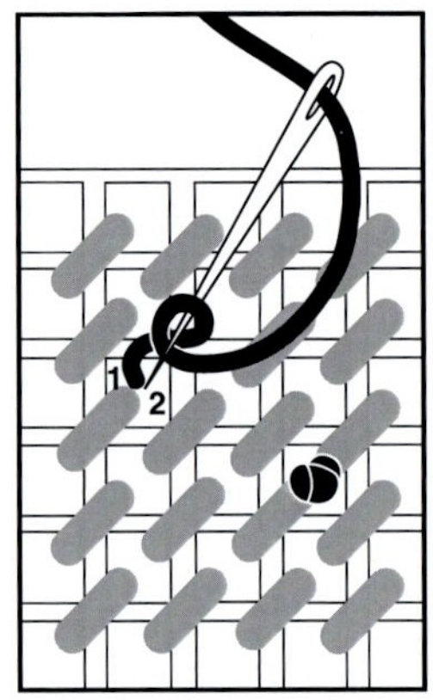

Fig. 8

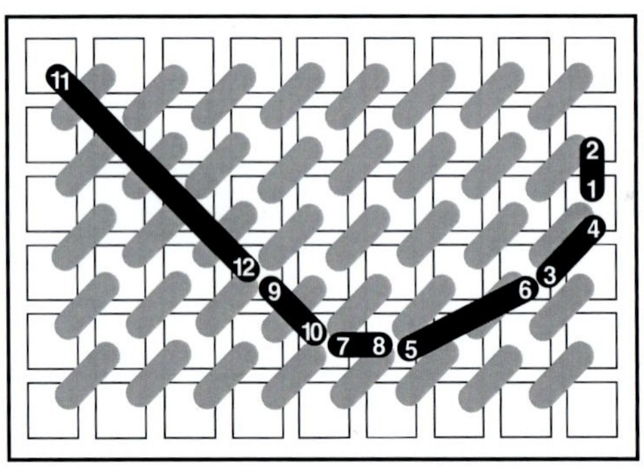

Fig. 7

Fig. 9

Production Team: Publishing Manager—Megan Copeland; Graphic Artist—Michael Douglas; Photo Stylist—Lori Wenger; and Photographer—Jason Masters.

Made in U.S.A.